Original title:
Mind Magic

Copyright © 2024 Book Fairy Publishing
All rights reserved.

Editor: Theodor Taimla
Author: Marlen Vesiroos
ISBN HARDBACK: 978-9916-756-92-8
ISBN PAPERBACK: 978-9916-756-93-5

Museum of Dreams

Through corridors where whispers gleam,
Imaginations unfurled,
In silent halls of magic beams,
Awaken a hidden world.

Portraits of hope and endless flight,
Memories sculpted in gold,
A timeless dance of day and night,
Within these walls so old.

Laughter crystallized in time,
Stories woven with light,
In this museum so sublime,
Every dream burns bright.

Shadows play with ghostly sheen,
Crafting tales untold,
In the Museum of Dreams unseen,
Mysteries unfold.

Step into this ethereal maze,
Where boundaries drift and blend,
Lost in the reverie and haze,
These dreams will never end.

Mystical Musings

Under skies of twilight's grace,
Whispers touch the soul,
Voices from a distant place,
Where secrets softly roll.

Stars align in cosmic sway,
Crafting visions deep,
In a realm where shadows play,
Silence takes a leap.

Nature's symphony in bloom,
Invokes a dreamy trance,
In the heart of night's dark room,
Stars in silence dance.

Mystic realms of whispered lore,
Timeless, ageless, bold,
Unlocking heaven's hidden door,
Mysteries unfold.

Drifting through these endless streams,
Thoughts in twilight's hold,
In the land of mystical dreams,
Ancient tales retold.

Sorcery of Silence

In stillness, the world transforms,
Silent spells take flight,
Through quiet whispers, magic forms,
In the calm of night.

Shadows waltz with gentle grace,
In the sorcery of peace,
A calmness fills the sacred space,
Where all turmoil cease.

The moonlight casts a silver glow,
Enchanting the unknown,
In silence, ancient secrets flow,
In hushed, eternal tone.

Truths emerge from quiet's core,
Like soft, enchanting chime,
In silence, one can hear much more,
Beyond the chains of time.

In this realm where quiet reigns,
Mystery aligns,
Sorcery of silence gains,
A power so divine.

Symposium of Souls

In the echo of twilight's song,
Souls begin to gather,
Whispers soft and time drawn,
Conversations lather.

Old and new in spectral dance,
Stories weave and twine,
A symposium of happenstance,
In this realm divine.

Ghostly figures share their plight,
In shadows softly blurred,
In the flicker of the night,
Every voice is heard.

Boundaries of time dissolve,
In this sacred space,
Where eternal morrows solve,
Mysteries we chase.

Join this commune, spirit bright,
Where ancient wisdom flows,
In the symposium of night,
Every secret shows.

Eclipsed Perception

In shadows cast, the twilight's breath
Whispers secrets of the day
Hidden truths beneath night's sheath
Eclipsed sight will find its way

Veiled in dreams where visions played
Silhouettes of unseen light
Silent whispers softly swayed
Guiding paths through darkest night

Ghostly shades in moonlit hues
Dance upon the spectral stage
Eyes that see through veiled views
Unlock the soul's encrypted page

Through the void, perception clefts
Navigating hidden streams
In the space where light berefts
We uncover hidden dreams

Curtains lifted, sight restored
In the eclipse, we found more
Truth and dreams in visions stored
Eclipsed sight, an open door

Psychic Sorcery

Mind's eye in realms of mystic
Reaches far beyond the veil
Ancient spells in forms cryptic
Unveiling futures to unveil

In the depths of midnight's lore
Weaving threads of fate unseen
Whispers from the evermore
Cast in spells both pure and keen

Visions shimmer, ethereal
Echoes of a time unknown
Power bound in rites primal
Reality, by dreams re-sown

Through the cosmos, spirits glide
Scrying truths from starlit script
Intuition, mystic guide
Reality through magic gripped

In this web of psychic might
Past and future intertwined
Guided by the spectral light
Psychic sorcery refined

Reflective Runes

In ancient stones, truths engraved
Symbols of the ages past
Wisdom by the Fates bequeathed
Runes through time itself to last

Mirror of the soul's deep quest
Glimpse into the arcane lore
Mysteries in meaning dressed
Whispered as in days of yore

Etched in earth with sacred hand
Runes that shine like stars in night
Guiding hearts to understand
Reflections born in mystic light

In their forms, the secrets lie
Ancient tongues of silent grace
Pathways where the spirits fly
Truths revealed in starlit trace

Reflective runes, a cosmic guide
Mapping destinies unknown
With their light, the soul's allied
In their wisdom, journeys sown

Charms of Awareness

In the realm where thoughts reside
Whispers of the silent mind
Little charms like stars collide
Weaving truths by fate aligned

Through the fog of conscious stream
In the stillness, clarity
Charms of ancient wisdom gleam
Soul perceives with rarity

Each a spark of insight pure
Illuminates the shadowed night
Consciousness by charm unsure
Begins to see with inner sight

Glimmers of reality
Woven in the silent heart
Crafting dreams from unity
Mind, body, spirit, part

Awareness bound in charm's own thread
Perception's dance in cosmic rhyme
Guided by the truths once said
Eternal in the warp of time

Enigma of Awareness

In shadows deep of sentient mind,
Where echoes of the unknown bind,
A labyrinth of thoughts unwind,
In cryptic pathways intertwined.

Awareness whispers silent plea,
In realms of dark uncertainty,
A riddle locked with hidden key,
In depths of self's obscurity.

Through twilight's veil, a glimmer seen,
In moments rare, a lucid dream,
A fleeting grasp of what may seem,
Yet swiftly fades into the stream.

Questions dance in infinite play,
Unanswered truths in misty sway,
The enigma dawned with each new day,
A mystery that leads astray.

In searching eyes, a spark alights,
A quest through endless days and nights,
The flame of knowledge ever fights,
To pierce the enigma's shrouded heights.

Ethereal Whispers

From twilight's cusp, where shadows blend,
The whispers on the breeze ascend,
In tones that neither break nor bend,
A tale from realms where silence wends.

They sing of worlds where spirits fly,
On gossamer wings through starlit sky,
With secrets held in whispered sigh,
As age-old echoes drift on by.

Their murmurs trace through mystic air,
An otherworldly, fleeting prayer,
Of dreams unseen, and visions rare,
That weave in night's ethereal lair.

Through whispered words in shadowed nook,
A language lost to time's own book,
Yet those who listen, and who look,
May find its trace in nature's crook.

So heed the call of whispers light,
In darkened calm of softest night,
For in their song, the soul takes flight,
To dance with stars, pure dreams in sight.

Sorcery of Synapses

Within the cortex, magic lies,
Electric webs beneath the skies,
A sorcery that never dies,
In neural networks, sparks arise.

Like lightning in a stormy sea,
The synapses ignite with glee,
A dance of thought so wild and free,
An enigmatic energy.

Communion through the darkened void,
In pulses rapid, thoughts deployed,
Ideas crafted, old destroyed,
In patterns endless, thought alloyed.

A brainwave bursts, a comet sends,
Through galaxies of mind it rends,
In waves the arc of thought descends,
A cascade where no tether ends.

Thus in the mind, where logic bends,
The sorcery of synapse blends,
A complex spell that each portends,
The dreams with which the soul contends.

Spirit in Thought

In quiet depths, where thoughts reside,
Where conscious whispers softly bide,
The spirit in the mind does glide,
Through dreams and fears it does confide.

Beyond the veil of light and dark,
It leaves upon the soul its mark,
A guiding force, an unseen spark,
That shines through doubts, so starkly stark.

In moments still, when silence reigns,
And thoughts flow gently, freed from chains,
The spirit in the thoughts sustains,
A tranquil peace, where wisdom gains.

Through winding paths of memory,
An endless search for what may be,
The spirit navigates the sea,
Of conscious thought and reverie.

So let your mind in calm be sought,
Where every dream, and lesson's taught,
Can merge in meaning, finely wrought,
The journey of the spirit in thought.

Dreamer's Canvas

Upon the strands of twilight's weave,
Brush strokes in a sea of dreams,
Whispered thoughts in shadows breathe,
Reality is not what it seems.

A palette born of starry night,
Imagination knows no bounds,
With hues that shimmer, bold and bright,
In silent sleep, what dreams are found.

From faintest spark to raging fire,
Colors blend and voices say,
On dreamer's canvas, hearts aspire,
To capture night and twine with day.

Portal Reflections

In mirrors deep, the portals gleam,
Reflecting worlds beyond the glass,
With every glance, another dream,
A whispered echo from the past.

Through liquid light and shimmering air,
The passage opens wide and clear,
To realms unknown, a mindful dare,
To step beyond, or stand in fear.

In portals' depths, the future calls,
Reflections dance and twist the night,
Within those frames, a spark enthralls,
The journey starts, with pure delight.

Secret Labyrinth

Within the maze of winding thought,
A labyrinth of silent prayer,
Paths untaken, dreams are caught,
With shadows deep in corners rare.

Through hedges high and pathways thin,
The secrets kept, the whispers spun,
A quest for those who might begin,
To find the heart where all roads run.

In hidden turns and turns anew,
The truth reveals in light's embrace,
The maze, it shifts as seekers do,
Yet all return to find their place.

Ghostly Thoughts

In quiet halls of memory's keep,
Where shadows softly come to play,
The ghostly thoughts arise from sleep,
To dance before the light of day.

They whisper truths of long-lost time,
Of loves and fears and dreams once told,
A spectral song, a haunting rhyme,
That in our hearts forever hold.

Through misty veils, they come and go,
Unseen, yet felt in every breath,
For in the mind, they gently flow,
The silent echoes after death.

Heralds of Thought

In twilight's gentle whisper,
Ideas begin to form,
Like whispers of an unseen wind,
The mind's own quiet storm.

Each spark a tiny beacon,
Illuminates the dark,
Heralds of thought arising,
From ember to a spark.

They dance like phantom shadows,
On edges of the night,
Crafting worlds from the void,
In the absence of light.

And with each passing second,
A story starts to weave,
A timeless dance of reason,
In the night's deep reprieve.

Oh, heralds of our dreaming,
You guide us through the gray,
In your silent, subtle speaking,
You show us the way.

Veins of Light

Through the fabric of the morning,
Threads of light appear,
Weaving golden canopies,
Dispelling night-born fear.

Each ray a vivid lifeline,
Coursing through the sky,
Veins of light rekindling,
The dreams heart left to fly.

They trace the hidden pathways,
Of days still left unseen,
Glimpses of tomorrow,
In a luminescent sheen.

Invoking realms of wonder,
Awakening the new,
Veins of light revealing,
A world baptized in dew.

Guiding through the shadows,
Into destiny's sight,
Crafting dawn and dusk anew,
With every vein of light.

Mirrors of the Psyche

In the quiet depths within,
Mirrors start to gleam,
Reflecting all our hidden selves,
In a waking dream.

Glimpses of forgotten pasts,
And futures yet untold,
Mirrors of the psyche's realm,
In silvered depths unfold.

Each reflection tells a tale,
Silent, deep, profound,
Secrets of the heart unveiled,
In the quiet found.

They show us endless facets,
Of the soul's own flight,
Mirrors of the inner world,
In the darkest night.

Embrace the visions offered,
By these mirrors true,
For in those silent images,
We find ourselves anew.

Esoteric Symphonies

In the whispers of the wind,
An ancient song is spun,
Esoteric symphonies,
Beneath the rising sun.

Each note a secret language,
From times long passed by,
Echoes of the universe,
In a cosmic lullaby.

They weave unseen connections,
Through realms of thought and dream,
Celestial compositions,
In a soft, celestial stream.

A harmony of mysteries,
Resonates the spheres,
Esoteric symphonies,
Heard beyond the years.

Bathe in these pure moments,
Let the music weave,
Esoteric symphonies,
In the heart, believe.

Exquisite Ephemera

Whispers of moments, fleeting, serene,
Flickering shadows in soft light's gleam,
Echoes of laughter, vanished, unseen,
In time's embrace, a tender dream.

Petals that fall in a soft gentle sway,
Songs of the past in the winds play,
Ephemeron's dance in a transient display,
Fades with dawn, the night's sweet decay.

Beauty sways in ephemeral grace,
Tracing the moments we cannot replace,
A glimpse of the heart in a whispered space,
Dispersed like fog without a trace.

Echoes of days in memories bloom,
Waltzing in twilight, dissolving too soon,
Transient glories, like a pale moon,
Fading from day to a forgotten tune.

Glimmer of starlight, fleeting and bright,
Falling like rain in the velvet night,
Moments so brief, in a delicate flight,
Exquisite ephemera, lost to sight.

Subconscious Scrolls

In dreams, we wander secret lanes,
Silent whispers, unknown terrains,
Truths unfurl in shadowed strains,
A mind's script, where mystery reigns.

Winding paths through mental mist,
Images merge and thoughts twist,
Reality's grasp gently dismissed,
Subconscious scrolls in a sleepless tryst.

Fragments of time in a fractured scene,
Mirror reflections, oddly serene,
Woven with threads of the unseen,
Subtle pictures in a twilight sheen.

Whispered stories in shadow and light,
Crafted in the silence of night,
Ethereal realms in delicate sight,
Dreams illuminate with a soft light.

Ink of thoughts that softly flow,
Hidden tales only we know,
In the mind's garden, wandering slow,
Subconscious scrolls where secrets grow.

Charmed Within

In the chamber of the heart's soft hold,
Lies a charm, precious and bold,
A spell of love, like stories retold,
In whispers and warmth, forever unfold.

Eyes that speak in a silent grace,
Gentle touch in a heartfelt space,
Soul's reflection in an embrace,
Charmed within, a timeless trace.

Magic in moments, woven fine,
Threads of joy in a delicate line,
Hand in hand, our stars align,
In the dream of love, divine.

Sweet symphony in a lover's tone,
Together, never truly alone,
Bound by a charm we've always known,
In the heart where love has grown.

Charmed within, where magic lies,
In shared smiles and tender sighs,
In love's embrace, as life flies by,
A charm that never dies.

Mental Maze

Winding thoughts in a labyrinth line,
Pathways obscure, dimly shine,
Searching for answers, a hidden sign,
In a mental maze, enigmas define.

Shadowed turns in the mind's expanse,
Seeking clarity in each glance,
Hopes intertwined in a silent dance,
Lost in a maze of happenstance.

Voices whisper, echo, and fade,
Clues in the darkness, gently laid,
Threads of thought intricately played,
In the maze where the spirit strayed.

Moments of clarity break through,
Revealing the path anew,
In the mental maze, thoughts construe,
Patterns shift with a changing view.

Navigating through the shadowed haze,
Mindset's journey in a complex phase,
Answers found in the winding ways,
Solace within the mental maze.

Imaginative Vortex

In the swirl of vibrant dreams,
A canvas painted by whims,
Ideas dance in twilight beams,
In the mind's unbounded streams.

Colors merge and softly blend,
Whispers of the unknown send,
Echoes of thoughts without end,
Through this vast creative trend.

Wandering stars and moonlit spells,
Craft tales no verse compels,
In this world where fantasy dwells,
Imagination's fountain swells.

Reality's threads wear thin,
Weaving wonders deep within,
Boundless realms begin,
Where endless fictions spin.

Here, the ordinary transforms,
Breaching mundane norms,
Breeding surreal forms,
In imaginative storms.

Twilit Contemplations

Beneath the sky's serene expanse,
In twilight's silent dance,
Thoughts traverse in trance,
Beyond the night's advance.

Stars awaken in velvet guise,
As the daylight softly dies,
Questions in the dark arise,
Echoes of ancient ties.

Moonlight spills in gentle streams,
Upon the heart's quiescent dreams,
In the stillness, what redeems,
Glimmers of unseen themes.

Each shadow whispers lore,
Untold tales from days of yore,
In twilight's gentle score,
Mysteries forevermore.

Time's passage felt, yet unseen,
In twilight's placid sheen,
Moments held in between,
Where pondering hearts convene.

Psyche's Potion

In the chalice of the mind,
A concoction pure, divine,
Mystic brews of every kind,
Blend in thoughts, intertwine.

Wisdom's tinctures, dreams' elixirs,
Stirred by time in fervent mixers,
Potent swirls of hopes and fixtures,
Crafting life's profound mixtures.

Memories like aged wine,
Restore the spirits in decline,
Each drop a tale, a sign,
Of human hearts, the sacred shrine.

Emotions blend, a complex brew,
Known by sages, known to few,
In sips of joy, in sorrows too,
Psyche's potion, ever true.

By the moon's ethereal light,
This potion gleams, pure delight,
Guiding souls through the night,
Toward dawn's redeeming sight.

Mental Maze

Through corridors of thought we trace,
A labyrinthine, complex place,
Echoes of our minds embrace,
In an ever-changing space.

Paths entwine and bifurcate,
Twisting through this mental state,
Decisions that we contemplate,
Forge the future, write our fate.

In the maze we search, we strive,
Questions bold and truths arrive,
Curiosities contrive,
To keep the spark of life alive.

Some dead ends, some open doors,
New insights on the labyrinth's floors,
Mental mazes weave and bore,
Until our minds forever soar.

Each corner turned reveals anew,
Hidden clues to sift through,
Mapping out what is true,
In the maze of mind, we persue.

Alchemy of Awareness

In the crucible of time, thoughts align,
Transforming shadows into gold divine.
Perceptions blend, evolve and refine,
Crafted with care, they intertwine.

In the realm where daydreams gleam,
Reality bends: a fluid stream.
Awareness sparks, ignites the theme,
Unveiling truths that gently teem.

Consciousness shifts, a mystic dance,
In every glance, a second chance.
Whatever was shall rise, enhance,
In this alchemy, perceptions prance.

Layers of essence, deeply unfurl,
In the fabric of the inner world.
Each thread a thought, each pearl a swirl,
Of light within, where visions twirl.

In these moments, subtle, grand,
Understanding takes its stand.
Awareness blooms, by heart's command,
Alchemy wrought by mind and hand.

Twilight Cognition

In twilight hours, thoughts take flight,
Brushstrokes of dusk merge with night.
Imagination swirls in fading light,
Whispers of dreams in tranquil sight.

Cognition dances, shadows weave,
Ideas form, as night deceives.
In twilight's grip, perceptions cleave,
To fragments that the mind retrieves.

Waves of thought, gentle caress,
Twilight's veil, a soft impress.
Ephemeral truths, the mind confesses,
In silence deep, ideas ingress.

Hues of twilight, blending hues,
Mind explores, awakes, reviews.
In quiet moments, insights muse,
Boundless realms, they gently cruise.

In the twilight of cognition's stream,
Ideas shimmer, softly gleam.
With every dusk, a new regime,
Of understanding, like a dream.

Bard of the Brain

Bard of thoughts, inspired flows,
Crafting verses where wisdom grows.
In mental realms, where insight glows,
Rhyming tales of highs and lows.

From synapse sparks, a bard is born,
Penning lines with passion sworn.
In every thought, a truth ornate,
Stories of the mind's grand fate.

Epiphanies in phrases curl,
In mental layers they unfurl.
Bard of thoughts, in endless whirl,
Captures essence in a pearl.

Synaptic dance, a rhythmic beat,
Mind's own echoes, thoughts repeat.
Tales from depths, profoundly sweet,
In cerebral notes, they gently meet.

Bard of brain, continue on,
In endless night, approach the dawn.
With every word, boundaries drawn,
In your verses, we are gone.

Philosopher's Enchantment

In shadows deep where thinkers tread,
Philosophies in mind are bred.
With every thought, a new path spread,
Enchantments of the mind are fed.

Mystery in questions posed,
Answers hidden, yet disclosed.
Philosophical enchantments host,
A quest where reason never slows.

In reflections, truth conceals,
Philosopher's charm in layers reveals.
Through musings subtle, wisdom heals,
Perceptions shift, the soul feels.

Mind's enchantment, thought's embrace,
In every question, find your place.
Philosophic dance, sweet grace,
Leading hearts through time and space.

With every pondering, deeper delve,
Unlocking shelves within oneself.
Enchantments beckon, truths compel,
In philosophy's ancient spell.

Introspective Incantations

In the quietude of night
Answers flicker into sight
Shadows cast on ancient walls
Echoing the heart's own calls

In the mirror of the mind
Hidden treasures we may find
Whispers of a distant past
Merge with questions yet unasked

Twilight thoughts and silent dreams
Flow like ever-giving streams
Mysteries of self unfold
Brave the journey, brave the cold

Through the veils of inner space
Weaving threads of time and grace
Every doubt dispels a fear
Future paths becoming clear

From the shadows break to light
Dark to dawn within one's sight
Embrace the ebb, embrace the flow
For in the mind, all truths grow

Cognitive Constellations

Stars aligned in mindful skies
Truths revealed through patient eyes
Galaxies of thoughts afire
Guide our spirits ever higher

Cosmic patterns, mental dance
In the vastness, we advance
Every synapse lights the way
Toward the promise of new day

Neurons blaze like comet tails
Charting paths through hidden trails
In this cosmic mental spree
We decode our destiny

Heavens in our minds entwine
Concepts turning into signs
Mental orbits, bright and vast
Hold the keys to futures cast

Wonder in cognitive flights
Where the mind illuminates nights
Floating through this starry maze
Towards the dawn's enlightening rays

Bewitched Reflection

Through the glass, a vision shines
Worlds within these thoughtful lines
Mirrored truths and mirrored lies
Entangle deep behind the eyes

Potent shadows passed unseen
Fleeting as a midnight dream
In reflections, truths reside
Halos in which thoughts abide

Motion swirls within the pool
Chaos, calm in cosmic rule
Echoes of what might have been
Weave through thick and weave through thin

Figures fading into mist
Stories that the soul has kissed
By the edge of knowing's brink
Quivers thought on what to think

From this bewitched mirrored view
Come the shadows, come the new
In reflections find the key
Unlock truths to set you free

Cerebral Chants

Whispers in the mind's abyss
Chanting secrets like a kiss
Echoed songs in silent halls
Where each thought and vision calls

Litanies of inner cries
Reaching peaks and knowing highs
Silent hymns within the brain
Sung through joy and sung through pain

Intonations soft and low
In the mind, they come and go
Flowing with each beat of heart
Music that sets worlds apart

Deep within cerebral streams
Lies a matrix of our dreams
Verses that ignite the soul
Guide us to that distant goal

In these chants, our mind's delight
Darkness bends to clearest light
Listen well, these inner rhymes
Sing through ages, sing through times

Wizards of the Inner World

In caverns deep within our mind,
Where shadows dance and secrets bind,
There wizards cast their silent spells,
And whisper tales that time compels.

With arcane words and nimble thought,
They wrought realms where dreams are bought,
In realms unseen, their wisdom gleams,
Crafting worlds from distant dreams.

A hidden lore that we must find,
In labyrinths of soul entwined,
Where memories and mystics swirl,
The wizards of the inner world.

Their magic stirs the soul's delight,
Illuminates the darkest night,
Unfolds the truth in symbols curled,
The wizards of the inner world.

Oh, guardians of thoughts so deep,
In reveries where secrets keep,
Through inner worlds, we're gently hurled,
By wizards of the inner world.

Enigmatic Reflections

In mirrors cracked, where shadows play,
Reflections mask the light of day,
A myriad of faces peer,
Through glass they beckon, ever clear.

An echo of a Life untold,
In silver panes, a tale unfolds,
Shimmering veils of truths unseen,
Enigma's dance on surfaces sheen.

Through looking glass, our thoughts abide,
A whispered truth that cannot hide,
Fragments of a soul's confession,
In enigmatic reflection.

Mirrors hold the mysteries old,
Stories lost and myths retold,
In their depths, a secret lies,
With whispered dreams and silent cries.

Through gleaming glass our spirits dive,
Seeking truths that thoughts derive,
Enigma's light within the night,
In reflections, hidden bright.

Sorcery of Synapses

Electric magic, neurons light,
In twilight thoughts, a spark ignites,
Sorcery of synapses revealed,
Unfolding worlds through thoughts concealed.

Connections weave a tangled thread,
In minds where ancient mystics tread,
Each current flows through paths untrod,
In brain's embrace, the dance of gods.

With every synapse, wisdom flows,
A secret language only knows,
In circuits born of energy,
The sorcerer's silent symphony.

Through labyrinths of thought's design,
Where reason's stars and logic shine,
Each spark, a spell that casts the night,
A tapestry of endless light.

Neural wizards weave their lore,
In endless dance forevermore,
Synaptic spells, a silent sea,
Of consciousness and mystery.

Metaphysical Reverie

In dreams where time and thought converge,
Beyond the scope of worldly urge,
A journey through the stars unseen,
In metaphysical, serene.

Whispers of the cosmos' call,
In reverie, we start to fall,
To realms where reason takes its leave,
And purest fantasies conceive.

A place where logic's bounds do fade,
Into the mists where dreams are made,
The universe's silent plea,
In metaphysical reverie.

Worlds within where secrets hide,
In cosmic dance horizons wide,
Unfold the truths beyond our sight,
In dreams that shimmer through the night.

A journey past the edge of now,
In inner space, we make our vow,
To cherish all that thoughts decree,
In metaphysical reverie.

Invisible Notes

In the stillness of night, they play,
Notes unseen, in quiet sway.
Whispers weave through moonlit air,
A melody beyond compare.

Stars above, they hum and dance,
Casting dreams in astral trance.
Every breeze, a hidden chord,
Nature's symphony adored.

Softly strum the strings of time,
Eternal tunes, profound and prime.
Harmony in shadows cast,
Echoes from a distant past.

Listen closely, hear the song,
Invisible, it won't be long.
Heartbeats keep the rhythm true,
Unseen music, me and you.

Silent chorales, in darkness bloom,
Infuse the night with soft perfume.
Invisible notes of love and light,
Guide us gently through the night.

Sorcerous Synapses

In the mind's enchanted space,
Neurons spark in mystic grace.
Electric thoughts in arcane dance,
Casting spells with every chance.

Mental currents surge and weave,
Forms of magic they conceive.
Whispers of forgotten lore,
Pulse within, forevermore.

Alchemy of brain and soul,
In every synapse, visions scroll.
Enigmas burst in spectral hue,
From depths of consciousness, anew.

Cosmic wisdom, lightning fast,
Through neurons, ancient spells are cast.
Mental realms in secret flight,
Dreams ignited, pure delight.

With sorcerous threads, our minds are spun,
Infinite puzzles, never done.
Within our heads, a mage's map,
Worlds awakened with each snap.

Insight's Whisper

A quiet voice within us speaks,
Where silence flows and reason seeks.
In moments still, the whisper grows,
Revealing truths that one must know.

Glimpses caught in gentle breeze,
Thoughts alight like autumn leaves.
A tender nudge, a subtle clue,
Guiding hearts to paths anew.

Mysteries unfold in silent folds,
Ancient wisdom gently holds.
In the hush, a beacon bright,
Insight whispers through the night.

Soft as shadows, firm as stone,
Inward journeys undertaken.
Wisdom's light within us gleams,
Silent whispers, endless dreams.

In every soul, a voice profound,
Guides us when there's none around.
Listen close, and you will find,
Insight's whisper, pure and kind.

Spellbound Synapses

In cerebral realms where wonders blend,
Synapses fire, old turns to mend.
Hey diddle diddle, the neurons twiddle,
Within gray matter's magic spindle.

Sparks of thought in neural dance,
Forge realities at every chance.
Each connection, a spell anew,
Weaving dreams in vivid hue.

Electric pulses bind and twist,
Creating realms of unseen mist.
In every spark, a world is born,
With every breath, new visions sworn.

Wizards of the mind, we are,
Crafting spells both near and far.
A synaptic spellbound trance,
In this brain-bound magic dance.

Thus we dwell in mental light,
Bound by spells both day and night.
Enchanted is the mind's deep space,
Live we shall in its embrace.

Mystic Brainwaves

In silent depths of night, we swim,
Thoughts morph in shadows, soft and dim,
A whisper's touch, a silent hymn,
We drift in waves at reason's rim.

In quiet tides, our minds engage,
A play of light on conscious stage,
Through hidden trails, an endless maze,
We dance within this cosmic cage.

Ideas bloom like cosmic streams,
A surge of colors, endless dreams,
We ride the currents, what it seems,
Is only glimpses, fleeting gleams.

Mystic waves we can't contain,
In realms where logic bears no reign,
We touch the stars, dissolve the pain,
In mental seas, where dreams remain.

In twilight's glow, our thoughts align,
A symphony without design,
Within these waves, so pure, divine,
Our minds explore the vast, the fine.

Dreamweaver's Craft

In threads of silver, dreams entwine,
A tapestry of stars design,
In slumber's grasp, their patterns fine,
Within our minds, they softly shine.

With every whisper, night unfolds,
A realm where endless story holds,
We wander paths of tales retold,
In crafted dreams, our fates are bold.

The dreamweaver's hand, so light, precise,
Spins fiction's web, beyond device,
In visions vast, where thoughts suffice,
We journey forth, through realms concise.

In sleep's embrace, creation springs,
With every dream, new hope it brings,
From silent depths, where soft voice sings,
We rise on woven, whispered wings.

In darkness deep, a spark ignites,
A world of wonders, boundless sights,
Within this craft, where no one fights,
We find our truths in shadowed nights.

Secret Synapses

Where thoughts in hidden circuits spark,
A dance unseen within the dark,
In silence deep, they leave their mark,
On neural paths, profound, stark.

Beyond the veil of conscious mind,
Where secrets lie in webs entwined,
In electric arcs, their truths we find,
Connections vast, and yet confined.

Patterns form, like stars in skies,
Unseen by waking, grounded eyes,
In whispering winds where knowledge flies,
A symphony of silent cries.

Through hidden realms, where logic flows,
A secret language only grows,
In every pulse, a mystery glows,
In synaptic dance that no one knows.

In night's embrace, they softly weave,
Connections deep, that never leave,
In every thought, we must believe,
In secret synapses, we perceive.

Phantom Perceptions

In shadows cast by twilight's gaze,
A world unseen begins to phase,
Where phantom thoughts, in quiet praise,
Emerge from mind's forgotten maze.

Amid the whispers of the past,
Perceptions, fleeting, form at last,
In moments brief, where shadows cast,
Impressions faint, yet holding fast.

Through veils of mist, where senses blend,
A dance of thoughts begins to send,
Illusions drift, and visions bend,
In phantom dreams, we find a friend.

In silent rooms where echoes play,
Perceptive ghosts begin to sway,
In realms where night and thought convey,
Unknown desires, hidden away.

Within the mind, where shadows creep,
Phantom nods in silence keep,
They guide us through the waking sweep,
To secrets held in unseen deep.

Whispers of Thought

In the quiet of night, dreams softly spin,
Mysteries unfolding from the realms within,
Silent musings, like stars, begin,
Whispers of thought, where stories akin.

Echoes of memories softly glow,
Through the mind's labyrinth, they flow,
Carving paths where shadows grow,
A dance of follies, above and below.

Silken threads in the wind's caress,
Unveil secrets we dare not express,
In the heart's chamber, they coalesce,
A cryptic verse we cannot repress.

Moonlight beckons to the weary soul,
Guiding steps to a hidden goal,
In dreams, we find our pieces whole,
Whispers of thought, a whispered scroll.

In twilight's embrace, we find our place,
Where time concedes to a gentler pace,
Thoughts intertwine in a delicate lace,
In the ethereal dance, we find our grace.

Invisible Strings

Through the ether, connections unseen,
Invisible strings delicately glean,
Binding hearts in a tender sheen,
Bridging worlds where wishes convene.

Voices carried on the breath of air,
Whispers of love in the shadows where,
Silent harmonies linger, rare,
In the unseen realm, we learn to care.

Tugging gently at our deepest core,
Unseen forces forevermore,
Invisible strings, a quiet lore,
Connecting souls as they explore.

In moments fleeting, we perceive,
The bonds that neither take nor leave,
Threads of fate, weaves that cleave,
Our stories, in silence, they conceive.

Though unseen, they firmly hold,
Invisible strings, stories untold,
Binding us with threads of gold,
Through the unseen, our lives unfold.

Enchanted Reverie

In a realm where the wild thoughts play,
An enchanted reverie, night and day,
Visions drifting in a golden ray,
Where dreams and reality softly sway.

Fields of wonder, vast and wide,
In this place, no truth can hide,
Whispers of magic, far and wide,
In enchanted reverie, we confide.

Colors burst in a silent storm,
Shapes and shadows, they transform,
In this dreamscape, lush and warm,
Enchantments swirl in endless form.

Every wish, a star reborn,
In twilight's light, our spirits adorn,
Guided by an unseen horn,
Through reverie's path, we are sworn.

Beyond the veil, a world we see,
Limitless as the deepest sea,
In this lucid fantasy,
We live our enchanted reverie.

Conscious Alchemy

In the twilight where thoughts conspire,
Lies a realm where dreams aspire,
Within the heart's eternal fire,
Conscious alchemy, raising higher.

Elements of fate, deftly spun,
In the alchemist's touch, they're one,
Transforming beneath the setting sun,
Where consciousness and soul are spun.

Mysteries blend in a sacred brew,
Turning the old into brand new,
Through hidden rites, the seeker knew,
Alchemy's touch in a golden hue.

In every thought, a seed is sown,
Where wisdom's light has brightly shone,
From lead to gold, the spirit's tone,
Conscious alchemy, the seeker's own.

In the crucible of time's embrace,
We find our truth in endless space,
Crafting essence with gentle grace,
Through conscious alchemy, we trace.

Invisible Enchantment

Silent whispers weave through the air,
A symphony no one else can hear.
Magic dances on the unseen breeze,
Mystic melodies, strange and clear.

Shadows cast illusions, soft and light,
Phantoms flutter in moonlight's glow.
Veils of night conceal the truth,
Mysteries only the dreamers know.

Eyes closed tight yet visions come,
A world within a world unfurls.
Enchantments hide in common sights,
An unknown realm of hidden pearls.

Invisible threads of fate entwine,
Binding hearts with spells so rare.
The unseen force, unspoken bond,
Secrets held in the quiet air.

Beyond the veil where mortals dream,
An enchantment lies, unseen, profound.
A subtle charm, a gentle spell,
A magic silently all around.

Cognitive Charms

Ideas glisten, a web of light,
Threads of thought in a midnight sky.
Mind's lantern shines through the dark,
Illuminating where the answers lie.

Intricacies of the human mind,
Synaptic sparks that leap and dance.
Cognitive threads weave conscious cloth,
Each fleeting glance a knowing chance.

Whispers of wisdom softly speak,
In the silence of a wandering mind.
Charms of cognition gently spark,
Where logic and mystery are intertwined.

In the depths of a thoughtful sea,
Concepts rise like morning tide.
Waves of understanding crest,
To reveal the truths they hide.

Cognitive charms, invisible chains,
Bind thoughts in a harmonious flow.
Through the labyrinth of the mind,
Wisdom's pathways subtly glow.

Intrigue of Insight

Behind the veil of what is seen,
Lies the world of pure insight.
Where knowledge blooms like hidden flowers,
In the shadowed corners of the night.

Curiosity seeds the fertile mind,
Questions sprout and branches curve.
Insight grows in silence's hold,
Where the thinkers' hearts preserve.

Soft epiphanies suddenly dawn,
Light within the deepest dark.
Mysteries unravel in quiet hours,
As insight ignites a spark.

The universe whispers secret truths,
To those who listen with keen ears.
Intrigue in the whispered winds,
Dispelling all the mortal fears.

A tapestry of thought unfurls,
Intricately woven, bright.
In the quiet, the brave find,
The endless intrigue of insight.

Arcane Intellect

Beyond the grasp of simple minds,
Lies intellect both vast and arcane.
A labyrinth of boundless thought,
Where ancient wisdoms still remain.

Echoes of time in silent halls,
Hushed whispers of the scholar's lore.
The arcane art of knowing all,
Within the pages bound in yore.

Celestial charts and cycles traced,
Patterns in the cosmic dance.
Intellect seeks the hidden truth,
Through the universe's expanse.

Philosophers' stones of ancient thought,
Alchemies of the cerebral kind.
Arcane keys to unlock the gates,
To treasures that the wisest find.

In the sanctum of the quiet mind,
Lies intellect that years refine.
Arcane deep, insight profound,
Eternal quests in thoughts divine.

Ponderous Portals

In realms where whispers weave through night,
Ancient doors creak in twilight's sight.
Mystic keys in spectral hands,
Unlock worlds in shifting sands.

Through veils of dreams, the seeker strides,
Echoes whisper where truth abides.
Shadows dance in hidden halls,
Secrets beckon with silent calls.

Beyond the gate, a timeless space,
Contours of an unseen grace.
Wisdom pours from depths unseen,
In this mosaic, a tranquil scene.

Phantasms float on ether's flow,
Inward journeys, where thoughts go.
Ever searching, minds contend,
With ponderous portals at night's end.

The key twists in silken light,
Revelations born from night.
Eyes awaken, spirits mend,
In pathways where dreams transcend.

Whispers of the Cerebral Enigma

In corridors where silence reigns,
Mysteries pulse through thought's terrains.
Veiled riddles in subconscious streams,
Nurturing the heart of dreams.

Synapses spark with hidden fire,
Thoughts rise where insights conspire.
A labyrinth of silent lore,
Every whisper, a map implore.

Unfolding layers, depths reveal,
Cerebral puzzles ours to feel.
Through whispers past the mind's expanse,
Truths align in shadow's dance.

Neurons hum with spectral flare,
Sifting through the thin-veiled air.
Whispers echo, soft, profound,
In the cerebral enigma found.

Drifting in the spaces between,
Moments merge where thoughts convene.
Wisdom whispers in twilight's gleam,
Unlocking echoes of the dream.

Sorcery of Thought

Woven threads of silent stream,
In the loom where ideas gleam.
Casting spells with ink and quill,
Sorcery's touch, the mind to thrill.

Imagination's arcane art,
Potions brewed in the thinker's heart.
Spirits rise in whispers thin,
Where sorcery and thought begin.

Stars align in cerebral sky,
Casting shadows where questions lie.
Wisdom circles, orbits high,
In the sorcery of a dreamer's eye.

Enchanted words in twilight melt,
Binding worlds with visions felt.
Sorcerers of thought's domain,
Crafting realms where dreams remain.

Ephemeral and yet profound,
Echoes of wisdom, circling 'round.
Sorcery of thought unfurled,
Binding magic in our world.

Labyrinths of the Psyche

Within the mind, vast mazes spin,
Corridors where dreams begin.
Twisting paths that take their flight,
In shadows of the inner night.

Echoes from the distant past,
Ghostly whispers, shadows cast.
Winding roads through thoughts obscure,
Mysteries in labyrinths pure.

Beneath the conscious, secrets seep,
Where ancient echoes gently creep.
Twilight paths through hidden spheres,
Labyrinthine, yet none to fear.

Connections form a web unseen,
Resonating in a silent sheen.
Depths of psyche play their role,
In the labyrinth of the soul.

Journeys through the winding night,
Seeking wisdom, seeking light.
In the psyche's vast domain,
Labyrinths weave through joy and pain.

Mysterious Mirth

In shadows deep where moonlight sprays,
Laughter hides in secret ways,
A giggle whispers through the night,
Fleeting, like a bird in flight.

Stars above with eyes aglow,
See the mirth in dark below,
Mysterious, this joy unknown,
Seeds of joy by dusk are sown.

Mirthful spirits in the shade,
Dance till morning starts to fade,
Their chuckles rise with morning's birth,
Enchanting hearts with mysterious mirth.

Spellbound Senses

Soft whispers float on twilight's breeze,
Enchanting senses with such ease,
Spellbound are the ears that hear,
Melodies both far and near.

Eyes are drawn to gleaming stars,
Diamond lights in sky-bound jars,
A vision steals the breath away,
With magic songs the night will sway.

Touch is warmed by firelight's glow,
Gentle kisses, soft and slow,
Bound by spells that time suspends,
In a night that never ends.

Hidden Realms

Beyond the veil of mortal sight,
Lie realms concealed from day's bright light,
In twilight's grip, their secrets bloom,
In silence of the midnight gloom.

A whispered name, a shadow's trace,
Leads seekers to a hidden place,
Where rivers shimmer, stars descend,
To worlds where dream and truth can blend.

These hidden realms, with doors unshown,
Invite the heart to roam alone,
In lands where magic softly streams,
We find the path within our dreams.

Thought Enchantment

Within the mind where thoughts take flight,
Enchantment weaves through day and night,
A spell of wonder, words unspun,
Begins where consciousness has won.

Through labyrinths of mind's own lore,
Ideas float, explore, implore,
Each thought a whisper, soft and kind,
In silent tapestries they bind.

Illusions form, realities blend,
As thoughts enchanted never end,
In realms enriched by dreams, uncharted,
A spell of thought is thus imparted.

Illusions of Perception

Mirrors fling the shadows wide,
Reflections twist and hide the truth.
Eyes deceive where mind preside,
What we see, a fleeting sleuth.

Colors blend in twilight's clasp,
Whispers ride on winds unknown.
Phantom shapes in moonlight's grasp,
Mysteries of evening's tone.

Distant stars in waters dance,
Ripples kiss the mirrored night.
Dreams received in trance's chance,
Faint illusions, tricks of light.

Glinting sparks in summer's haze,
Mirage forms in golden glow.
Faith and doubt in tandem graze,
Fleeting scenes in mind's tableau.

Hollow echoes, sight's delight,
Subtle tricks our senses spin.
Through the veil of shadowed night,
Do we see what lies within?

Wonders of Wit

Levity in words we weave,
Smiles draw in clever play.
Puzzles in our minds believe,
Day turns bright from banter's ray.

Chuckles form from nimble tongues,
Riddles wound with jest and tease.
Heartfelt laughter softly sung,
Joys released in winks with ease.

Wit adorns the baneful night,
Lights the darkest paths we tread.
Quips and jests apposed with might,
Guard the heart from deepest dread.

Quickened thoughts in playful sway,
Sparkling like the morning dew.
Charmed as if by faerie's lay,
Every jibe and jest born new.

In clever verve, life's wonders found,
Crafted words, a potent spell.
Laughter's voice in joy unbound,
Echoes where the light hearts dwell.

Inner Mystique

Depths unseen in quiet mind,
Silent whispers, shadows cast.
Thoughts like veils of moonlight find,
Truths beneath the questions vast.

Hidden tides of dark and light,
Waves of hope and doubt profound.
Inner realms of endless night,
Where our secret dreams are crowned.

Mystic signs in whispered rain,
Threads of fate in humble guise.
Glimpses caught through fleeting plain,
Of the soul's elusive ties.

Voices soft from ages past,
Echoes in the twilight air.
Wisdom in the shadows cast,
Guided by a silent prayer.

Veiled in thought's enshrouded halls,
Mystique deep within the heart.
Where the quiet spirit calls,
Binding all the worlds apart.

Thoughtful Conjuring

Imagination's realm so vast,
Flights of fancy, visions spin.
Magic in the thoughts we cast,
Dreams arise and dance within.

Words like wands with potent power,
Crafting worlds from blushing air.
Every phrase a petal flower,
Blossomed forth with deftly care.

Mind's eye paints with vivid hues,
Whispered winds and starlit seas.
Fantastical in different views,
Shaping all the mind decrees.

Thoughtful spells in silence weave,
Conjuring life from still repose.
Mysteries where ideas cleave,
In the fertile mind that grows.

Wonders born from notions deep,
Crafted forms by inner light.
In these dreams our hearts will keep,
Endless stories through the night.

Cerebral Symphony

In echoes of thought, a melody starts,
Rhythmic pulses from mind to heart.
A chorus of ideas, soaring high,
In the cerebral sky, they freely fly.

Harmony of neurons, synaptic dance,
Ideas born from a single glance.
Silent symphony of the inner mind,
Endless pathways, all intertwined.

Verses of logic, tunes of dream,
Flowing like a crystalline stream.
A world within, vast and grand,
Conducted by an invisible hand.

Imagination's orchestra, playing free,
Infinite compositions, come to be.
Notes of reason, chords of delight,
Filling the canvas of mental night.

In this hall of the intellect's prime,
A symphony that transcends time.
Ephemeral yet forever true,
A cerebral symphony, just for you.

Unseen Whispers

From corners where shadows softly play,
Unseen whispers weave night to day.
In the hush of a silent breeze,
Secrets dance amongst the trees.

Voices of the past softly drift,
Through time's ethereal rift.
Silent stories, ancient and old,
In whispers, their truths are told.

Gentle breezes carry sage advice,
Unseen whispers, silent and nice.
Knowledge hidden in the quiet night,
Gleaming in the dim twilight.

Across the starlit, whispered sky,
Thoughts in whispers softly fly.
Veiled murmurs of hope's embrace,
In unseen whispers, find their place.

Hidden truths in the quiet hum,
From silent voices, wisdom comes.
In the secrets of the murmuring air,
Unseen whispers, always there.

Whirlwind of Wisdom

In the storm of thoughts that never cease,
Whirlwind of wisdom, moments of peace.
Spiraling insights, deep and profound,
In the chaos, true wisdom is found.

Torrents of knowledge, torrents of grace,
Whirlwind of wisdom in fleeting embrace.
Through the turbulence, clarity grows,
In the whirlwind, the truth always shows.

Amidst the gale of mindful storm,
Insights and lessons take form.
Gales of wisdom, fierce and bright,
Guiding through the darkest night.

Tempest of thoughts, wisdom's grace,
In the whirlwind, we find our place.
Eternal whirl of learning's sway,
Path of wisdom, lights our way.

Cycles of intellect, endless spin,
Whirlwind of wisdom, begins within.
In the eye of knowledge, calm and true,
Infinite wisdom, born anew.

Empyreal Ruminations

In realms beyond the earthly sight,
Empyreal ruminations take flight.
Thoughts ascend to the cosmic sphere,
Whispers of the divine draw near.

Celestial musings, vast and grand,
Touching realms we cannot understand.
In starlit silence, wisdom gleams,
Empyreal ruminations, like dreams.

From the heavens, insight flows,
Secrets that the universe knows.
In the quiet of the highest skies,
Thoughts of eternity softly rise.

Ethereal musings on life's core,
In empyreal thoughts, we explore.
Cosmic truths in tranquil flight,
Guiding through the darkest night.

Beyond the stars, where thoughts are free,
Empyreal ruminations decree.
In the vast expanse, clear and bright,
Our souls find their guiding light.

Nebulous Thoughts

In the twilight of the mind,
Fleeting dreams begin to wind,
Clouds of wonder softly sway,
Whispers of a distant day.

Glimmers fade in murky shadow,
Hopes and fears in ebb and flow,
Undefined in silent trance,
They waltz in cryptic dance.

Echoes of a time unknown,
Through the corridors, they've flown,
Phantoms of the abstract kind,
Ephemeral, they intertwine.

Cryptic Reflections

In the mirror, shadows play,
Secrets kept from light of day,
Silent whispers, heart concealed,
Mysteries that won't be revealed.

Eyes that gaze with hidden pain,
Truths that ripple, yet remain,
Depths of soul in veiled sight,
Chasing fragments of the night.

Dual faces, light and dark,
Every scar a hidden mark,
Cryptic echoes, mind confined,
Seeking peace, yet never find.

Arcane Ruminations

Midnight musings take their flight,
Through the realms of misty night,
Mystic runes and ancient lore,
Secrets whispered evermore.

Veils of smoke, obscured trails,
Tales of yore in moonlight pales,
Patterns writ in starlit skies,
Arcane thought in guise of lies.

Labyrinths of winding past,
Echoes deep and shadows cast,
Lost in time's uncharted space,
Wisdom drifts with silent grace.

Quixotic Quanta

Dreams of splendor, wild and free,
Riding winds of mystery,
Particles in endless dance,
Caught within a fleeting glance.

Visions in a quantum haze,
Boundless night and boundless days,
Infinite in wild defiance,
Quixotic worlds in their alliance.

Cosmic whispers, spacetime thread,
Tales untold and words unsaid,
Chance and fate in wild ballet,
Spin the dreams of night to day.

Spirit of Thought

In twilight's gentle, mystic light
Ideas take ethereal flight
With moonbeams casting shadows bright
Mind's muse awakens in the night

An unseen force begins to weave
A tapestry we can't conceive
Yet in our hearts, we dare believe
To this, our spirits all cleave

Wander through the astral plane
Where thoughts like raindrops fall as rain
Each idea, a link in the chain
Insight gained, never in vain

In every whisper of the breeze
Comes a truth that sets us at ease
Borne on nature's endless seas
Thought and spirit find their keys

The soul and mind, in balanced stride
With stars to guide us far and wide
In realms where deep insights reside
Our thoughts and spirits are allied

Charmed Cortex

Within the mind's enchanted maze
Golden dreams in twilight blaze
Each neuron sparks and gently plays
In a dance that night conveys

Illusions form, then softly melt
Shaping worlds we've never felt
In corners where the shadows dwelt
Our senses sharpened, deeply dealt

In synapse fire, ideas emerge
Like tidal waves that gently surge
Through thought's vast ocean, we diverge
On the brink of logic's verge

Imagination's tender spell
From conscious bounds, we bid farewell
Inward journeys we compel
To the depths where insights dwell

Charmed cortex, with magic rife
Entangles dreams with waking life
A mystic place, devoid of strife
Where visions cut like a knife

Nexus of Notions

In the nexus where thoughts collide
Imagination's doors swing wide
A place where dreams and facts abide
And wisdom's river does reside

Here, whispers of the ancient past
Guide future's hand, steady and fast
Each moment, a spell must cast
To bind the knowledge that will last

Mind's echoes blend, a vast array
Of unformed sparks, a bright bouquet
In twilight shades of dusk and day
New notions find their shining way

Concepts span from dusk to dawn
Through mental fields, we wander on
In search of truths to pin upon
Our spirits' canvases long drawn

Nexus of notions, boundless space
Where endless thoughts find their place
Each idea, an endless chase
Within this boundless mental grace

Enochian Elucidation

In celestial tongues, whispers grow
Secrets of the stars bestow
Upon the mind, a gentle flow
Of ancient wisdom, soft and slow

From angel's lips, the truths descend
In words that time itself can't bend
Unseen forces, realms transcend
On pathways where the spirits wend

Glyphs of light, in ether drawn
Illuminate the darkest dawn
Mysteries of the ages gone
By enochian spells are shown

Discerned in sacred, silent night
Are visions far beyond our sight
By arcane symbols burning bright
Our souls are cast in purest light

Enochian truths, a sacred lore
Reside within us evermore
A bridge to realms we must explore
To the divine, our spirits soar

Psychic Spellbook

In ancient tomes of hidden lore,
A whisper spills from page to air.
Mystics conjure, evermore,
Dreams and visions, rarest fair.

Stars align and secrets rend,
Mystic circles, power bind.
Wielding realms, we can't amend,
Spirit echoes in the mind.

Whispered words and sacred signs,
Interweave in twilight's hem.
Veins of ether, myst'ry's vines,
Bond the stars in cryptic gem.

Candles burn in silent rhyme,
Letters glow, and runes entwine.
Ancient echoes through all time,
Weaving spells of pure design.

With each page anew awakes,
Worlds unseen, where shadows play.
Psychic force in words that shake,
Opening to realms astray.

Mirage of Memory

In desert's breath, a vision gleams,
Of yesteryears, a fleeting glance.
Mirage of memory, woven dreams,
A spectral dance, a fleeting trance.

Sands of time slip through our hands,
Moments fade like twilight's end.
Echoes etched in shifting sands,
Forever lost, yet still they blend.

Faint impressions, shadows cast,
Mind's mirage, in twilight's glow.
Reflections of a distant past,
In memory's stream, they ebb and flow.

Figures drawn in hazy light,
Ephemeral and softly blurred.
Phantoms of long-gone nights,
In whispering winds, their song is heard.

Chasing phantoms of yore,
Through deserts vast of time and space.
Mirage of memory, evermore,
A vanished world we still embrace.

Ghosts of Wisdom

Ancient whispers, knowledge deep,
Through the ages, voices seep.
Shadows from the past arise,
Ghosts of wisdom, truest spies.

Riddles hidden in their breath,
Echoes of the timeless sage.
Silent specters cheat their death,
Words of wisdom on life's stage.

Books unopened, scrolls unfurled,
Guardians of secret thought.
Haunted corridors, they're swirled,
Wisdom's ghosts have ever taught.

Eyes that see through eons wide,
Knowledge clings to spectral frame.
In their truths, we must confide,
Legends long, yet still the same.

From the shadows, insights bloom,
Ghosts of wisdom softly tread.
Guiding candles in the gloom,
Lighting paths of those they've led.

Intellectual Incantations

Words of power, minds awake,
Incantations thought ignites.
Through the ether, visions break,
Casting forth in knowledge lights.

In the labyrinths of thought,
Wisdom blooms from hidden seeds.
Concepts cradle what they're brought,
Incantations the mind feeds.

Arcane whispers fill the air,
Ideas dance in mystic trance.
Intellects beyond compare,
Spirits rise in thought's expanse.

The quill's touch, a magic spark,
Transforms thoughts to written spell.
Ideas grow in shadows stark,
Each word cast weaves knowledge well.

In the chambers of the mind,
Ancient spells of thought are cast.
Intellectual bonds combined,
Hold the future, forge the past.

Cerebral Fantasia

In the labyrinths of the mind, dreams fly,
Hovering like starlit clouds in the sky,
Ideas like meteors, in swift array,
Pathways of thought in endless play.

Imagination weaves tapestries bold,
Infinitesimal treasures, stories untold,
Mirrored reflections of what might be,
In a cerebral dance of creativity.

Thoughts intertwined like ivy's embrace,
Lost in the timeless quantum of space,
Ephemeral whispers, echoes that sing,
A fantasia of the inner being.

Rivers of notions, rivers of light,
Guiding through the nebulous night,
Minds unshackled, find their own sea,
In the boundless fields of mental spree.

Cascades of wisdom, gently unfold,
In cerebral realms, wisdom behold,
A symphony of intellect, endlessly spins,
Beginnings and ends, where fantasy begins.

Seraphic Insights

A whisper in the twilight's calm descent,
Angelic voices, divinely sent,
Guiding hands through life's perilous sea,
Seraphic insights, wild and free.

Wings of light and halos bright,
Guardians of the sacred night,
Spirits unseen, with eyes so clear,
Pour secrets in a mortal ear.

Soft as the dew upon morning grass,
Messages of the heavens pass,
In gentle tones that hearts discern,
A truth that makes the spirit burn.

In visions pure with golden hue,
A celestial touch, tender and true,
Eyes uplift to realms of grace,
Where seraphic whispers find their place.

Transcendent flames in soft caress,
Unfold the path to happiness,
In seraph's glow, the soul perceives,
The wisdom that the heart believes.

Fantastical Gears

Turning, churning, the intricate dance,
Of brass and copper, shadows prance,
Of cogs and springs, a symphony,
In the heart of a grand machinery.

Tick-tock, the gears in concert sing,
A marvel of mechanical ring,
Spirits bound in metal's embrace,
In a realm where time finds its place.

Whispers of oil in the axioms glide,
Mirrored wonders in their stride,
Lost in the maze of mystic levers,
Dreams unfurled by iron weavers.

Clockwork dreams in a spiraled bend,
Pathways linked that never end,
Harmony found in every spin,
Fantastical realms crafted within.

Crank and twist, in lively cheer,
The hum and whir of a purpose clear,
In the pulse of clockwork gears,
Fantastical wonders yet to steer.

Currents of Perception

In the waters of thought, I drift and sway,
Currents of perception guide the way,
Echoing whispers of depth unknown,
In the soul's river, silently sown.

Perception dances in ripples of light,
Glimmering truths in the shadow of night,
Reflections cast on the water's rise,
Moments where reality wears a disguise.

Eyes awaken to the shifting stream,
The ever winding, lucid dream,
Perceptions alter in fluid form,
Bridging thoughts through the mental storm.

Tides of insight, ebb and flow,
By the moon's gentle, mystic glow,
Visions in water, soft and clear,
Whispering secrets that only hearts can hear.

Floating free in perceptive seas,
Where the mind finds its keys,
Unraveling layers of the deep,
In the currents where mysteries sleep.

Wondrous Mirage

Beneath the scorching desert skies,
A world unfolds, a mystic prize,
Shifting dunes of golden grace,
Whisper secrets in this place.

Mirages dance in heatwaves tall,
Visions fleeting, shadows crawl,
In the distance, hope appears,
Quenching thirst of ancient fears.

Oasis hidden, yet so near,
Promises of waters clear,
Life in barren lands takes hold,
Stories in the sand are told.

Camels plod through endless ways,
Compass points to brighter days,
In this realm of sand and sun,
Journeys end, another's begun.

Here, the desert, wide and vast,
Sings of past and futures cast,
In the mirage, dreams converge,
Reality and myth emerge.

Veil of Contemplation

Silence falls like twilight's shroud,
Thoughts ascend, escape the crowd,
Veil of night's serene embrace,
Time to ponder, slow the race.

In these moments, wisdom breathes,
Through the rustle of the leaves,
Calm descends, the mind unveils,
Secrets whispered through the gales.

Stars ignite the tranquil skies,
Answers found in moonlit eyes,
Questions drift on evening breeze,
Echoes of eternal seas.

Heartbeats sync with nature's flow,
Wisdom gained in shadows' glow,
Mysteries of life unfold,
In contemplation, truths are told.

When the night begins to fade,
Dawning light resets the shade,
Knowledge gleaned in quiet's lore,
Guides the path forevermore.

Arcane Notions

In the labyrinth of time and space,
Lie secrets none can quite embrace,
Arcane notions weave their spell,
Mysteries where shadows dwell.

Symbols etched on ancient stone,
Languages of the unknown,
Wisdom hidden, cryptic, old,
Whispers of the truths untold.

Across dimensions thoughts traverse,
Tangled webs of the universe,
Patterned stars and cosmic dance,
Hints of destiny and chance.

Ancient runes and prophecies,
Chart the course of galaxies,
Arcane threads through history,
Binding past and yet-to-be.

Seekers of the mysteries,
Gaze into the cosmic seas,
Understanding, ever near,
Arcane truths await to hear.

Flight of Fancy

Upon the wings of whimsy soar,
Beyond the realms of slumbered lore,
In the land where dreams take flight,
Marvels dance in boundless light.

Castles rise in candy skies,
Dragons wink with knowing eyes,
In this world where thoughts unbind,
Fantasy and fate entwined.

Clouds of silk and rainbows' end,
Whispered breezes, visions send,
Through the realms of make-believe,
Every heart can dare conceive.

Adventures bloom with every breath,
Chased away the shades of death,
In this kingdom, wild and free,
Boundless realms of reverie.

Journey through the twilight's grace,
Magic found in every place,
Waking from this fancied flight,
Worlds remain within our sight.

Conjuring Cognition

In the depths of thought's abyss,
Minds weave webs, crafting bliss.
Ideas birthed in shadows' elation,
Conjuring new cognition's creation.

Whispers of neurons spark sight,
Consciousness takes flight.
Threads of reason finely bound,
In intellect's haven found.

Labyrinths of grey matter spin,
Worlds of logic lie within.
Enchanting spirits of the mind,
In knowledge's grasp, we find.

From chaos, order springs anew,
A vision born, a clearer view.
Wondrous, vast, the cerebral sea,
Endless realms of discovery.

Thoughts entwined in subtle dance,
In the heart of wisdom's trance.
Stars of insight brightly gleam,
In the forge of reason's dream.

Ethereal Intellect

Wisps of thought in twilight's glow,
Eternal truths begin to show.
Unveiling secrets of the night,
Ethereal intellect takes flight.

Specters of wisdom softly gleam,
Floating in the conscious stream.
Whispers of the ages past,
In the boundless, they contrast.

Beyond the veil, where muses play,
Ideas dawn, like breaking day.
Fragments of the infinite,
In realms the mind can only flit.

Sparks of clarity ignite,
In intelligence's gentle light.
Bound by neither space nor time,
Immortal, pure, and so sublime.

A dance of ethereal grace,
In the cosmos, minds embrace.
Transcendent, boundless, free,
The intellect's vast tapestry.

Psychic Alchemy

Alchemy of the psychic kind,
Transmute the fragments of the mind.
Secrets spun in thought's retreat,
In mental alchemy, we meet.

Turning leaden doubts to gold,
Mysteries of the spirit unfold.
Catalysts of dreams they find,
A philosopher's stone for the mind.

Brews of wisdom, potions deep,
Elixirs of insight we keep.
In labyrinths of thought concealed,
Truths arcane are then revealed.

Transformation's subtle art,
A revolution at the heart.
Power of the gaze within,
Seek the change, let it begin.

Here, in thought's crucible bright,
We forge new visions in the night.
Alchemists of the soul, we'll be,
In the dance of psychic alchemy.

Enchanted Contemplation

In the garden of the mind's flight,
Enchantments bloom in soft twilight.
Thoughts meander through the haze,
In contemplation's endless maze.

Whispers of an age-old spell,
In reverie, they softly swell.
Echoes of a silent lore,
Guardians of the mental door.

Meditative streams of thought,
Inward journeys, secrets sought.
Serenity in the calm embrace,
Of contemplation's gentle grace.

In shadows cast by inner light,
Ideas dance, so pure, so bright.
Mirrors of the soul's reflection,
Caught in mental introspection.

Dwelling in this enchanted trance,
Boundless thought begins to dance.
Exquisite realms of silent sound,
In contemplation's magic found.

Visionary Vortex

Amidst the ethereal twilight gleam,
Spirals of thought in a dream's stream,
Ideas twirl, with mind's embrace,
In this vortex, time and space.

Parallel realms in shadows lie,
Reflections of the star-kissed sky,
Mysteries weave in silent flow,
Infinite paths where few can go.

Visionaries dance in cosmic spin,
Boundless journeys where they begin,
Their steps trace echoes of the sun,
Each one's journey, a thread spun.

Fathomless depths where spirits soar,
Unlocking truths from ancient lore,
Timeless whispers in each twirl,
The visionary's quest unfurl.

Strands of light and dark entwined,
In this vortex, realms combined,
A canvas painted with bold hues,
Where souls explore and ideate anew.

Eldritch Echoes

Whispers in the midnight's glow,
Through veils where shadows flow,
Ancient tongues speak secrets dire,
Eldritch echoes, dark and higher.

In the stillness of the night,
Ghostly murmurs take their flight,
Unearthly chants from yesteryears,
Woven threads of phantomed fears.

Wandering through the spectral haze,
Lost souls in a timeless maze,
Their lamenting calls distill,
Echoes linger, haunting still.

Dim-lit realms where phantoms dwell,
Whispered secrets left to tell,
Arcane truths in voids they weave,
Dreams of worlds we can't perceive.

Fathomless eyes peer through the dark,
Eldritch chants leave their mark,
In silence, unseen spirits sing,
Of ancient rites and eldritch king.

Harmonious Haze

Morning mist on fields of green,
Softly whispers where muses dream,
Nature's symphony begins anew,
In a haze of harmonic hue.

Birdsong threads the waking air,
Melodic calls beyond compare,
Wind and leaves in gentle dance,
Forming nature's true romance.

Golden rays through dew-kissed veil,
Weave a tale in breezes frail,
Butterflies in silent flight,
Dance in the dawn's soft light.

Waters ripple in cadence tight,
Singing brook in morning light,
Each note blends in perfect phase,
Creating this harmonious haze.

Ephemeral yet eternally seen,
This harmonious waking scene,
A world where peace and beauty blaze,
In nature's timeless, gentle haze.

Secrets Unspoken

Silent thoughts in twilight held,
Words unspoken, feelings meld,
In the shadows where hearts confide,
Secrets in the soul reside.

Eyes that speak in muted hues,
Through reflections, hidden clues,
Longing whispers veiled in night,
Silent hopes that seek the light.

Furtive glances in the dark,
Unrevealed, leave their mark,
Unvoiced echoes that convey,
Words that falter, fade away.

Mysteries in every sigh,
Coded in the gazing eye,
Truths that linger, softly blend,
Secrets shared 'midst trusted friend.

In the silence, stories traced,
In the quiet, hearts embraced,
Till the dawn, where whispers woken,
Reveal the secrets long unspoken.

www.ingramcontent.com/pod-product-compliance
Lightning Source LLC
LaVergne TN
LVHW010552070526
838199LV00063BA/4953